Her Rainmaker
25 Proven Principles for Your Success

Ty Media Group Publishing™
127 W. Fairbanks Ave. Suite 102
Winter Park, Florida 32789

Her Rainmaker, 25 Proven Principles for Your Success©
First edition 2008 by Ty Young

ISBN: 978-0-9819085-8-8

Table of Contents

Her Rainmaker

Ty's Life Unscripted

Introduction

Ty Young was born and raised in Los Angeles, California. She is 1 of 2 girls born to a 15 year old mother and 17 year old father, themselves children. Ty found herself on her own at the age of 14 in a big city like Los Angeles, California.

Ty put herself through middle and high school where she eventually graduated high school. Through her adversity, she kept her ears and eyes open for opportunities. She was introduced to entrepreneurship by a friend at age 17. With a desire to be financially independent, Ty saw a niche that needed to be filled and opened a mom and pop pager and cellular phone business with just small savings. Purchasing phone numbers at $1 each and leasing the numbers to customers at $10-15.00 per month, at the age of 19, Ty's income exceeded $10,000 per month.

Ty has traveled extensively, and has lived in large urban centers establishing numerous small businesses in the industries of book publishing, music business, telecommunications, television production, technology, promotions, small business consulting and multimedia. Her current multimedia marketing and small business development company is currently thriving and successful. Ty has established businesses in Los Angeles, Washington DC, New York City, Atlanta, Jacksonville, Orlando and Miami, Florida.

The Choice

On my journey for success, it was imperative that I followed my intuition and not people. I was told on many occasions that I would never make it. Fortunately, I didn't choose to make people the center of my life. It would have been easy for me to make that choice being alone for so many years. My God given intuition showed me a different route. I chose to believe in the unseen and that was faith in the promises of God.

Ty Young

The Price Tag

Choosing to follow my spirit, I often found myself lonely, yet never without peace. I chose favor over a feeling. I saw favor as a bow tied around Grace being offered to me by Jesus himself. So I accepted the price tag and chose "Truth," the road less traveled.

Ty Young

25 Proven Principles for Your Success

Principle #1
Be Hot or Cold, Not Lukewarm

Revelation 3:15-16 (New Living Translation)

15 "I know all the things you do, that you are neither hot nor cold. I wish that you were one or the other!
16 But since you are like lukewarm water, neither hot nor cold, I will spit you out of my mouth!

Revelation:

When you are not clear or honest with another or yourself you become completely ineffective in your life and that of those around you.

Have Your Say

Principle #2
DBJ "Don't Be Jealous"

Genesis 37:18-20 (New Living Translation)

Joseph sold into Slavery

18 When Joseph's brothers saw him coming from a distance. As he approached, they made plans to kill him.
19 "Here comes the dreamer!" they said.
20 "Come on, let's kill him and throw him into one of these cisterns. We can tell our father, a wild animal has eaten him. Then we will see what becomes of his dreams!"

Revelation:

Envy and jealously creates division amongst friends and families. It's such a powerful emotion that it creates division amongst strangers.

Have Your Say

Principle #3
Keep It 1000%

John 8:32 (New Living Translation)

32 And you will know the truth, and the truth will set you free.

Revelation:

To withhold the truth from another is like stealing the sun from the sky on a cold day.

Have Your Say

Principle #4
Check Your Heart

Matthew 12:34-37 (New Living Translation)

34 You brood of snakes! How could, evil men like you speak what is good and right? For whatever is in your heart determines what you say.

35 A good person produces good things from the treasury of a good heart and an evil person produce evil things from the treasury of an evil heart.

36 And I tell you this; you must give an account on judgment day for every idle word you speak.

37 The words you say will either acquit you or condemn you."

Revelation:

"Walk in love," is a phrase that challenges you to judge a person with your heart and not your head. Your heart is the epicenter of your emotions. When faced with hate or envy we are required to have empathy for that person who inflicts their negativity upon us. To walk in love is equivalent to having compassion for our adversaries.

Have Your Say

Principle #5
If She Wins, We Win

1Timothy 5:2 (New Living Translation)

2 Treat older women as you would your mother, and treat younger women with all purity as you would your own sisters.

Revelation:

Women are the glue that holds together communities and families. With so much responsibility on their shoulders women are in need of much support. Unfortunately women are known to be catty, negative and untrusting, while men are known to stick together by any means necessary.

Many doors have been open for women due to the price many women have paid by giving their lives for their fellow women.

Have Your Say

Principle #6
Keep It Moving

Hebrews 12:1(New Living Translation)

1 Therefore, since we are surrounded by such a huge crowd of witnesses to the life of faith, let us, strip off every weight that slows us down, especially the sin that so easily trips us up. And let us run with endurance the race God has set before us.

Revelation:

Often we stay in relationships and friendships that should have ended sooner than later. The continuance of toxic relationships will lead to bitterness and anger. It's imperative to keep it moving once you have an opportunity to flee.

Have Your Say

Principle #7
Check Their Fruit

Matthew 7:16-20 (New Living Translation)

16 You can identify them by their fruit, that is, by the way they act. Can you pick grapes from thorn bushes, or figs from thistles?

17 A good tree produces good fruit, and a bad tree produces bad fruit.

18 A good tree can't produce bad fruit, and a bad tree can't produce good fruit.

19 So every tree that does not produce good fruit is chopped down and thrown into the fire.

20 Yes, just as you can identify a tree by its fruit, so you can identify people by their actions.

Revelation:

God gives us spiritual signs about others whether negative or positive. Many people refer to this as a gut feeling. If you don't believe that God has given you that spiritual intuition, the next best thing to do is to check their fruit. For example, if you meet a man that has five children by five different women, you should be alarmed by what his decisions have produced in his life as bad fruit produced by a fruit tree.

Have Your Say

Principle #8
Think Rationally Through Your Emotions

1 Samuel 25:32-38 (New Living Translation)

32 David replied to Abigail "Praise the LORD, the God of Israel, who has sent you to meet me today!

33 Thank God for your good sense! Bless you for keeping me from murder and from carrying out vengeance with my own hands.

34 For I swear by the LORD, the God of Israel, who has kept me from hurting you, that if you had not hurried out to meet me, not one of Nabal's men would still be alive tomorrow morning."

35 Then David accepted her present and told her, "Return home in peace. I have heard what you said. We will not kill your husband."

36 When Abigail arrived home, she found that Nabal was throwing a big party and was celebrating like a king. He was very drunk, so she didn't tell him anything about her meeting with David until dawn the next day.

37 In the morning when Nabal was sober, his wife told him what had happened. As a result he had a stroke, and he lay paralyzed on his bed like a stone.

38 About ten days later, the LORD struck him, and he died.

Revelation:

Love is an emotion that is sometimes compared to a state of insanity. Love is also called blind. Love is a feeling that if not monitored and due to the emotional reward received by the feeling can be extremely emotionally over-whelming.

This emotion usually dims the light of wisdom and understanding. Many have killed in the name of love. As any feeling or emotion that hinders our ability to think rationally love seems to be the most deadly of them all. This is what makes this principle so important. We need to think rationally through our emotions.

Have Your Say

Principle #9
Write Your Vision

Habakkuk 2:2-3 (New Living Translation)

2 And the LORD answered me, and said, "Write the vision, and make it plain upon tables, that he may run that readeth it."

3 For the vision is yet for an appointed time, but at the end it shall speak, and not lie. Though it tarry, wait for it; because it will surely come, it will not tarry.

Revelation:

Writing down your dreams and aspirations is like hanging up a sign that says, "Open for Business." Writing it down, you declare yourself in the game. Putting your vision on paper alerts the part of your brain known as the reticular activating the system to join you in the play.

Have Your Say

Principle #10
Kill the Disease to Please

Luke 10:38-42 (New Living Translation)

Jesus Visits Martha and Mary

38 As Jesus and the disciples continued on their way to Jerusalem, they came to a certain village where a woman named Martha welcomed him into her home.

39 Her sister, Mary, sat at the Lord's feet, listening to what he taught.

40 But Martha was distracted by the big dinner she was preparing. She came to Jesus and said, "Lord, doesn't it seem unfair to you that my sister just sits here while I do all the work? Tell her to come and help me."

41 But the Lord said to her, "My dear Martha, you are worried and upset over all these details!

42 There is only one thing worth being concerned about. Mary has discovered it, and it will not be taken away from her."

Revelation:

"The disease to please," is a form of addiction. Just as a drug addict seeks drugs, a people pleaser seeks approval. We should help others and try to make them happy. Give for the pleasure of giving. But, the need to please others at all cost at all times, and to be everything to everyone, are actions of a desperate person.

People pleasers are desperate people. Compulsive pleasing is different from an altruistic desire. Such a compulsion has serious physical and emotional consequences in the long term.

Have Your Say

Principle #11
God Is Your Source

Proverbs 10:22 (New Living Translation)

22 The blessing of the LORD makes a person rich,
And he adds no sorrow with it.

Revelation:

Provision and promise comes from God! God can use many avenues to bless you, but He is the ultimate source behind every blessing. Your job or occupation is one avenue God can use to bless you. But, your job is not your source.

God can bless you through friends and relatives, but they are not your source. Even if they fail you or forsake you, God will not.

Have Your Say

Principle #12
www.ZIPIT.com

Proverbs 10:19 (New Living Translation)

19 Too much talk leads to sin. Be sensible and keep your mouth shut.

Revelation:

The simple key to working well with others is to listen more and talk less. This is also one of the hardest, as people always feel the need to explain themselves or prove their point. Unfortunately, talking until you are blue in the face will get you nothing beyond a blue face.

A useful way to remember the proportion of listening to speaking is to remember that you have two ears and one mouth. Quite simply, you should listen twice as much as you speak.

Have Your Say

Principle #13
Business 1st Ladies

Proverbs 24:27 (New Living Translation)

27 Do your planning and prepare your fields before building your house.

Revelation:

When you build your business before you build your house you will develop self sufficiency in your finances. Without self sufficiency you will be in bondage to the person or persons who are in control over your finances.

Have Your Say

Principle #14
Guard Your Heart

Proverbs 4:23 (New Living Translation)

23 Guard your heart above all else, for it determines the course of your life.

Revelation:

The poet Maya Angelou wrote a poem to all of her Christian sisters that says, "A woman's heart should be so hidden that a man has to find God before he can get access to it."

Have Your Say

Principle #15
Position Yourself to Prosper

Ruth 3:1-15 (New Living Translation)

1 One day Naomi said to Ruth, "My daughter, it's time that I found a permanent home for you, so that you will be provided for.

2 Boaz is a close relative of ours, and he's been very kind by letting you gather grain with his young women. Tonight he will be winnowing barley at the threshing floor.

3 Now do as I tell you to take a bath and put on perfume and dress in your nicest clothes. Then go to the threshing floor, but don't let Boaz see you until he has finished eating and drinking.

4 Be sure to notice where he lies down; then go and uncover his feet and lie down there. He will tell you what to do."

5 "I will do everything you say," Ruth replied.

6 So she went down to the threshing floor that night and followed the instructions of her mother-in-law.

7 After Boaz had finished eating and drinking and was in good spirits, he lay down at the far end of the pile of grain and went to sleep. Then Ruth came quietly, uncovered his feet, and lay down.

8 Around midnight Boaz suddenly woke up and turned over. He was surprised to find a woman lying at his feet!

9 "Who are you?" he asked. "I am your servant Ruth," she replied. "Spread the corner of your covering over me, for you are my family redeemer."

10 "The LORD bless you, my daughter!" Boaz exclaimed. "You are showing even more family loyalty now than you did before, for you have not gone after a younger man, whether rich or poor.

11 Now don't worry about a thing, my daughter. I will do what is necessary, for everyone in town knows you are a virtuous woman.

12 But while it's true that I am one of your family redeemers, there is another man who is more closely related to you than I am.

13 Stay here tonight, and in the morning I will talk to him. If he is willing to redeem you, very well then let him marry you. But if he is not willing, then as surely as the LORD lives, I will redeem you myself! Now lie down here until morning."

14 So Ruth lay at Boaz's feet until the morning, but she got up before it was light enough for people to recognize each other. For Boaz had said, "No one must know that a woman was here at the threshing floor."

15 Then Boaz said to her, "Bring your cloak and spread it out." He measured six scoops of barley into the cloak and placed it on her back. Then he returned to the town.

Revelation:

"A man with a supply of ideas fears nothing, for he has become the master of his own fate." – Robert P. Crawford

The more ideas, inventions, and insights you create, the more ideas you will continue to find the opportunities that exist are endless. As one opportunity dries up look around, you will quickly see other ideas that rush to the forefront. Keep your eyes open for connections that everyone, but the most astute observer, completely misses. Look for ideas in your industry, outside your industry, at the mall at work and at home.

Have Your Say

Principle #16
Be a Forward Thinker

Proverbs 4:25 (New Living Translation)

25 Look straight ahead, and fix your eyes on what lies before you.

Revelation:

Once you find what motivates you, and then take the next step. Focusing your thoughts and your attention on one step at a time makes it easier to reach your goals. Stay open to all possibilities and ideas. Divine intervention will guide you, making opportunities available where none may have existed before. You may even see new ideas that you never thought were possible. Do not doubt. New ideas will come your way. Be thankful for them. Look at them with a beginner's mind, with alertness and enthusiasm. Then move on to the next step.

Have Your Say

Principle #17
Get Some Advice

Proverbs 15:22 (New Living Translation)

22 Plans go wrong for lack of advice; many counselors bring success.

Revelation:

Too often people are too proud (or too stubborn) to ask for directions in our journey through life. But asking for advice from a colleague accomplishes two things: first, you might get the answer you seek, and second, it says to the person you trust and respect their opinion. By confiding in an individual, the advisor becomes concerned with your best interests. This leads to mutual trust and respect between people.

When you are asked to offer advice to another, be as articulate and rational as possible. If you do not know the correct answer, do not fabricate advice or mislead the person. This will only shatter the person's trust in you. Instead, point him in another direction where he might find the answer he is seeking.

Have Your Say

Principle #18
Time Is Money

Proverbs 12:11 (New Living Translation)

11 Hard work means prosperity, only fools idle away their time.

Revelation:

Time is money. You can't slow down this outflow of capital. But you can get it to work for you if you can learn how to convert it into money or the things money can buy. Use your time wisely; make sure as you use it, value is in site. We often allow people to waste our time. Negative energy often robs us of our time. Be mindful of such a valuable asset.

Have Your Say

Principle #19
If Thy Hand Offends Thee, Cut It Off

Matthew 5:30 (New Living Translation)

30 And if your hand even your stronger hand causes you to sin, cut it off and throw it away. It is better for you to lose one part of your body than for your whole body to be thrown into hell.

Revelation:

Some people go through life miserable, not knowing that by changing how they think and what they think about can change the physical circumstances in their world. People constantly listen to other people's opinions and not to their inner self and so end up not traveling on their true path. If you listen to people's negative spewing enough, your inner mind will get into the habit of believing what these negative people dish out! This is mental self sabotage!

Have Your Say

Principle #20
Iron Sharpens Iron

Proverbs 27:17 (New Living Translation)

17 As iron sharpens iron, so a friend sharpens a friend.

Revelation:

There is a saying, "Your income is the average of the five people you hang out with most and your level of success is the average of the five people you hang out with most." If you look around, you'll probably notice that to be true.

So, what does it mean for you today...right now? It means that it's important for you to surround yourself with big thinkers, people who are moving, growing, learning, and succeeding as a way of life. When you're in the presence of big thinkers; you naturally gravitate toward bigger ideas and they encourage you to explore them.

Have Your Say

Principle #21
The "She Myth"

Proverbs 4:6-9 (New Living Translation)

6 Don't turn your back on wisdom, for <u>she</u> will protect you.
Love her, and <u>she</u> will guard you.
7 Getting Wisdom is the wisest thing you can do!
And whatever else you do, develop good judgment.
8 If you prize wisdom, <u>she</u> will make you great.
Embrace her, and <u>she</u> will honor you.
9 <u>She</u> will place a lovely wreath on your head;
<u>She</u> will present you with a beautiful crown."

Revelation:

The Bible refers to Wisdom as a she. That scripture in Proverbs should be a platform of a healthy self worth. A woman should know her worth. Self worth is important to the ultimate happiness you feel in your life because it is closely connected to your self esteem. If you suffer with low self esteem and low self worth, you could find yourself in some very difficult situations. Why do you think people with a low self worth end up attracting the wrong people in their life? For instance are you or anyone you know in a relationship that is obviously not right?

How often do you hear people asking the question, why do women stay in abusive relationships? This is not an easy question to answer. There can be many reasons. If you were to ask the person involved why, they probably could not give you a satisfactory answer. The usual reply is because of the kids, or I know deep down he loves me. For those on the outside it is hard to understand. Most women are so good at hiding the fact that they have low self worth, and they even convince themselves that they are in control. Nothing could be further than the truth. There is a famous line from a popular song, "how empty of me to be so full of you."

Have Your Say

Principle #22
Let Your Light Shine

Luke 11:33-35 (New Living Translation)

33 "No one lights a lamp and then hides it or puts it under a basket. Instead, a lamp is placed on a stand, where its light can be seen by all who enter the house.

34 "Your eye is a lamp that provides light for your body." When your eye is good, your whole body is filled with light. But when it is bad, your body is filled with darkness.

35 Make sure that the light you think you have is not actually darkness.

Revelation:

Draw from your bag of "inner light" qualities and have them become the essence of who you are as you apply them to your daily interactions. From this, you will begin to experience a much more positive existence. You will find yourself looking for ways to implement these qualities, learn not to dwell on the negative, and seek out ways to make a difference in your life and the lives of others. It is a way to step out of you and learn to love and appreciate the work and life that you have, even if they are not what you ultimately desire. In short, it is a way of living in the moment that will produce startling results.

Have Your Say

Principle #23
Renew Your Mind

Romans 12:2 (New Living Translation)

2 Don't copy the behavior and customs of this world, but let God transform you into a new person by changing the way you think. Then you will learn to know God's will for you, which is good and pleasing and perfect.

Revelation:

2 Corinthians 10:4-6 For the weapons of our warfare are not carnal but mighty in God for pulling down strongholds, casting down arguments and every high thing that exalts itself against the knowledge of God, bringing every thought into captivity to the obedience of Christ, and being ready to punish all disobedience when your obedience is fulfilled.

Satan's strongholds are thoughts. If the devil can get you to entertain his thoughts; fear, anxiety, doubt, apprehension, and so on, he can have a doorway to controlling your mind. He will put a ring in your nose and lead you around if you let him, but, we don't have to let him. The Word of God tells us how to be victorious. It shows us how to be more than conquerors in Him who loved us and gave Himself for us.

Have Your Say

Principle #24
Focus On the Blue Dot,
Not the Red Dot

Numbers 13:25-33 (New Living Translation)

25 After exploring the land for forty days, the men returned
26 to Moses, Aaron, and the whole community of Israel at
Kadesh in the wilderness of Paran. They reported to the
whole community what they had seen and showed them the
fruit they had taken from the land. Ironically only a few out
of thousands gave a good report.

27 This was their report to Moses: "We entered the land you
sent us to explore, and it is indeed a bountiful country a
land flowing with milk and honey. Here is the kind of fruit it
produces.

28 But the people living there are powerful, and their towns
are large and fortified. We even saw giants there, the
descendants of Anak!

29 The Amalekites live in the Negev, and the Hittites,
Jebusites, and Amorites live in the hill country. The
Canaanites live along the coast of the Mediterranean Sea
and along the Jordan Valley."

30 But Caleb tried to quiet the people as they stood before
Moses. "Let's go at once to take the land," he said. "We can
certainly conquer it!"

31 But the other men who had explored the land with him disagreed. "We can't go up against them! They are stronger than we are!"

32 So they spread this bad report about the land among the Israelites: "The land we traveled through and explored will devour anyone who goes to live there. All the people we saw were huge.

33 We even saw giants there, the descendants of Anak. Next to them we felt like grasshoppers, and that's what they thought, too!"

Revelation:

Look for the positive. No matter what the situation is, there is always a negative and a positive side of it. Sometimes, the positive may not be easy to see right off the bat, but if you look deep enough it is there.

Don't look for the negative when it isn't present. A lot of us always enter a situation "looking" for the negative. Woman this is for you. Ever entered into a relationship with the belief that, "all men are dogs?" So, you half expect your partner or spouse to cheat on you because you have the belief, that all men are dogs. Even though there is no evidence of him cheating, you search his pockets for phone numbers, follow him in an unmarked car to see what he is doing when he claims to be out with "the boys."

Or, you might hear there is going to be lay-offs on your job. You automatically believe that you are on the list of "pink slips." You spend your day, watching your boss out the corner of your eye. She or he goes behind closed doors and you are convinced they are plotting to get rid of you.

Or, you walk in a room of your "friends" and they stop talking. You automatically assume they were talking about you, because why else would they stop talking. STOP! Don't look for the negative when it isn't a definite fact, because when you seek the negative, you often find it more than not.

Have Your Say

Principle #25
Your Enemies Know Your Gift

Genesis 30:1-8 (New Living Translation)

1 When Rachel saw that she wasn't having any children for Jacob, she became jealous of her sister. She pleaded with Jacob, "Give me children, or I'll die!"

2 Then Jacob became furious with Rachel. "Am I God?" he asked. "He's the one who has kept you from having children!"

3 Then Rachel told him, "Take my maid, Bilhah, and sleep with her. She will bear children for me and through her I can have a family, too."

4 So Rachel gave her servant, Bilhah, to Jacob as a wife, and he slept with her.

5 Bilhah became pregnant and presented him with a son.

6 Rachel named him Dan, for she said, "God has vindicated me! He has heard my request and given me a son."

7 Then Bilhah became pregnant again and gave Jacob a second son.

8 Rachel named him Naphtali, for she said, "I have struggled hard with my sister, and I'm winning!"

Revelation:

Most people aren't aware how insidious the deadly sin of envy is. It is unhappiness at another's success, or according to Merriam-Webster's Collegiate Dictionary, Tenth Edition, it's a "painful or resentful awareness of an advantage enjoyed by another joined with a desire to possess the same advantage." The root word is often Latin invidia, but there is also a Greek word (phonetically) poneiros that means "evil eye." Interestingly, this word can also mean "devil." People can be envied generally because simply they're good at something. It is also, "Ill will pure and simple, the hatred of good because it is good."

Have Your Say

Resources

Spiritual Development Resources

Below is a list of resources that has helped me to become and practice being a woman of integrity and perfecting my love walk for Christ and an abundant life.

Joyce Meyer – www.joycemeyer.org
Paula White – www.paulawhite.org
Creflo Dollar – www.creflodollarministries.org
Dr. David Uth – www.firstorlando.com
TD Jakes – www.thepottershouse.org
A.R. Bernard – www.arbernard.com
Noel Jones – www.noeljonesministries.org
Joel Osteen – www.joelosteen.lakewood.cc
John Hagee – www.jhm.org
Rob Thompson – www.winninginlife.org
Rudolph Mckissick, Jr. – www.bethelite.org
Jamal Bryant – www.jamalbryant.org
Charles Stanley – www.fba.org
Jentenzen Franklin – www.jentenzenfranklin.org
TBN – www.tbn.org
Streaming Faith – www.streamingfaith.com

Additional Books by Ty Young

Instant Income Strategies for Small Business

To purchase this book log onto:
www.tymediagroup.com

www.herrainmaker.com

Instant Income Strategies for Book Publishing

To purchase this book log onto:
www.tymediagroup.com

www.herrainmaker.com

Educational Resources
Her Rainmaker University

Visit us at
www.herrainmakeruniversity.com

•

For income opportunities:
www.herrainmakernetwork.com

CPSIA information can be obtained at www.ICGtesting.com
Printed in the USA
LVOW130940280812

296247LV00001B/36/P